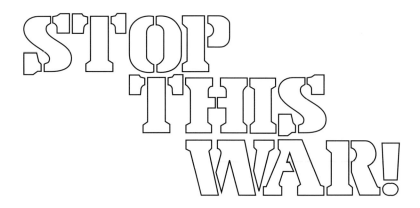

STOP THIS WAR!

STOP THIS WAR!

American Protest of the Conflict in Vietnam

Margot Fortunato Galt

LERNER PUBLICATIONS COMPANY • MINNEAPOLIS

To Ralph and Louise Galt, pacifist pioneers, and to their sons, Lester and Fran Galt.

A note on sources: I conducted a number of interviews to gather material for this book. Most of the people who kindly gave me their time and stories are named and quoted in the text. Specifically, I'd like to thank Fran Galt, Lester Galt, Robert Penn, Jim Moore, Anne Dodge Simpson, Bob Simpson, Lisa Boehlke, Alvin Odermann, Sue Lommen, Brian Nerney, Allen Hawley, and Dean Zimmermann. I owe them a debt of attention and honor for their memories and for making the choices they did during a turbulent, difficult time.

Lerner Publications Company
A Division of Lerner Publishing Group
241 First Avenue North
Minneapolis, MN 55401 U.S.A.

Website address: www.lernerbooks.com

Library of Congress Cataloging-in-Publication Data

Galt, Margot Fortunato.
      Stop this war! : American protest of the conflict in Vietnam /
Margot Fortunato Galt.
          p. cm.
      Includes bibliographical references and index.
      Summary: A social history of the protest by United States citizens against the Vietnam war, from the days of the first American involvement in Vietnam in the early 1960s through the 1970s.
      ISBN 0-8225-1740-X (alk. paper)
      1. Vietnamese Conflict, 1961–1975—Protest movements—United States—Juvenile literature. [1. Vietnamese Conflict, 1961–1975—Protest movements.] I. Title.
DS559.62.U6G35   2000
959.704'308—dc21
                                                            99-29554

Manufactured in the United States of America
1 2 3 4 5 6 – JR – 05 04 03 02 01 00

Contents

PACIFIST GENERATIONS

Make love, not war.
—Slogan of 1960s radical youth

In April 1964, Francis Galt stopped at his dorm mailbox in Frontier Hall at the University of Minnesota in Minneapolis. Fran, a freshman, was enjoying the excitement of the huge campus; the student population of 40,000 was 400 times larger than his hometown in North Dakota. Following a family tradition, he had quickly joined political organizations such as the Young Democrats, Students for Integration, and the Student Peace Union.

He had also, reluctantly, registered for the military draft. Begun during the Civil War and continued on and off ever since, the draft called young men into the U.S. Army, Navy, Marines, and other branches of military service when they turned 18. Unless they were deferred—or excused—for education, poor health, or family need, they had no choice but to serve.

The business envelope Fran drew out of the mailbox had a return address of the Selective Service System, Draft Board, Audubon, Iowa. Fran's parents had moved to Audubon, and he knew immediately what was inside—a small white draft card calling him to military service in South Vietnam, a country in Southeast Asia. Suddenly, a phantom gun was wedged against his shoulder.

THE ROCK AND ROLL OF CHANGE

By the time Fran Galt was opening his mailbox that day in 1964, U.S. military involvement in Vietnam was already a decade old. Presidents Dwight D. Eisenhower and John F. Kennedy had sent 25,000 advisory troops to South Vietnam to train that nation's soldiers. The United States was not yet involved in a full-scale war in Vietnam. But the conflict would eventually become the longest war in U.S. history.

In the early 1960s, Americans were redefining their country's role at home and abroad. A glamorous young president, John F. Kennedy, had called on every American to "ask not what your country can do for you. Ask what you can do for your country." He had created the Peace Corps, which trained young volunteers to work in poor countries around the world.

At home, African Americans were fighting for Civil Rights and an end to segregation and discrimination. On August 28, 1963, at the March on Washington for Jobs and Freedom held in Washington, D.C., Civil Rights leader Dr. Martin Luther King Jr. had made his fervent "I Have a Dream" speech. In the South, young people, black and white, put their ideals and their lives on the line to help desegregate schools, bus stations, and lunch counters and to help blacks register to vote.

The 1950s had been a conservative era. On college campuses, young women often wore neat "Peter Pan" collars, girdles, and high heels. Young men wore crew cuts and sports jackets. By contrast, in the early 1960s a wave of nonconformism began to sweep through college campuses, ushering in "long hair and beads or long hair and no beads," Fran said. "We shared a certain world view: antiwar, pro-equality—that is, equal races."

Young people listened to the rock and roll of Elvis Presley, to preppy white quartets like the Four Freshmen, and to smooth black groups like the Ink Spots. A new musical group on the scene—the Beatles from Liverpool, England—sang sweet songs but shocked conservative Americans with their long hair.

ORGANIZED FOR PEACE AND JUSTICE

Inspired by the Civil Rights movement and new cultural ideas, many young people got caught up in the spirit of change, protest, and political unrest. Many who protested followed the lead of their political parents. Some of them were old-time socialists and communists—people who believed that factories, land, and property should be owned in common by everyone in a nation. Others were pacifists—people who opposed war on religious or moral grounds.

Fran Galt's father, for example, had gone to prison during World War II to protest "all war." As a Christian minister, Ralph Galt could have gotten a deferment from the draft, but he refused. He would not cooperate with a system of killing nor take an easy way out that was not available to other men. He spent 21 months in a federal prison. Once released, he continued to protest war and racial injustice through the Fellowship of Reconciliation, an international Christian pacifist organization.

Ralph Galt's views on nonviolence and pacifism were "wrapped up in Christianity," as Fran put it, while Fran "had rejected organized Christianity by the time I was 18." Even so, Fran felt he followed his father's example. "I still believed in the philosophy of nonviolence," he explained.

So when Fran's draft card arrived, a wave of revulsion swept through him. There was no way he was going to support the military.

Closing the mailbox with its tiny window, he trudged upstairs, already thinking about the letter he would send to the draft board when he returned the card in protest. He expected to be jailed within the week.

DRAFT BOARDS AND CONSCIENTIOUS OBJECTORS

As soon as Fran returned his draft card, he expected an FBI agent to begin trailing him—as had happened to some leaders of radical organizations on campus. But none did. Fran's brother Lester had also spoken out against the draft. He had registered in North Dakota before the family moved to Iowa. North Dakota took a different way from the rest of the country, and as Fran put it, in the "grand North Dakota tradition of doing nothing," Lester's draft board did nothing.

Fran's Iowa draft board eventually sent him an application for conscientious objector (CO) status. As a CO, Fran could stay out of the armed forces, substituting two years of community service at home or in Vietnam for military service. Fran met many of the requirements

Fran Galt, **right,** *received his draft card while attending the University of Minnesota in Minneapolis. He first protested the war and the draft by returning it.*

for a CO: His family had a history of pacifism and his father was a minister. But Fran returned the CO application blank. Like his father, he refused to take an "out" that wasn't available to everyone. He wanted to resist the draft and protest all war.

His draft board asked him to visit and explain himself. "We met in a room in the courthouse," Fran remembered. "The men on the board knew my father. They assured me that they would approve my application for CO status if I would make it." But the meeting didn't last very long. "I wanted to outline my reasoning, but the draft board wasn't interested in listening," Fran recalled.

Soon after, Fran, his brother Lester, and many other young northerners went to Mississippi for the "Freedom Summer" of 1964. Their goal was to help enroll black Mississippians to vote. "In Mississippi we volunteers had a secondary role," explained Lester Galt. "Though we admired the Civil Rights leaders, we admired ordinary black people even more. The way they said 'This is my life, and I'm going to live it on my feet' affected us later. When we had a choice to make, we said, 'I'm not going to kill.'"

VIETNAM HEATS UP

For many young American men, that choice was fast approaching. On August 7, 1964, Congress passed the Tonkin Gulf Resolution, the result of clashes between North Vietnamese and U.S. ships in North Vietnamese waters. Though not an official declaration of war, the resolution allowed President Lyndon Johnson to "take all necessary measures to repel any armed attacks against the forces of the United States and to prevent further aggression" in Southeast Asia.

Only two senators voted against the resolution; the House of Representatives passed it unanimously. In a poll taken at the time, 85 percent of the American people supported the president's action. However, as James Warren wrote in *Portrait of a Tragedy: America and the Vietnam War*, "No historian has found any conclusive evidence of a North Vietnamese attack" on the Americans.

All of a sudden, Vietnam grabbed America's attention. Until this time, Vietnam was as unknown to most Americans as outer space. Suddenly people wanted to know what the fighting was about. They learned that in 1954, the French, who had previously governed Vietnam, had been forced out by the Vietnamese. Afterward, Vietnam was divided into two parts—North Vietnam under the leadership of Ho Chi Minh, a communist who had organized his people to defeat the French, and South Vietnam, governed by a series of leaders who had supported the French.

For 10 years the United States had been sending money and military advisers to help South Vietnam. By 1964 soldiers from North Vietnam were moving into South Vietnam and helping South Vietnamese peasants create their own army, the Vietcong (VC), to fight the South Vietnamese government. Without U.S. support, South Vietnam appeared destined to become communist like North Vietnam.

Throughout the 1950s, caught up by a fear of communism and the Soviet Union, the United States had been conducting an anticommunist crusade. The U.S. government was afraid that South Vietnam might become communist, too, and interfere with American trade and defense in Southeast Asia.

In February 1965, President Johnson ordered the bombing of North Vietnam. In March of that year, as part of "Operation Rolling Thunder," the first U.S. combat troops, 3,500 marines, arrived in Da Nang, South Vietnam. Soon General William Westmoreland, commander of the U.S. forces, would have 82,000 American men fighting under him.

A WAR IN ASIA,
A WAR AT HOME

It is a hideously immoral war. America is committing mass murder.

—Students for a Democratic Society, March on Washington, April 1965

Vietnam was the first war brought into American homes by television, and scenes of the war stunned the public. On the TV news, families saw helicopters whirring over flattened rice fields and straw huts going up in flames. Gone were the romantic, idealized images of Asia left by 1950s movies such as *Flower Drum Song* and *Sayonara.* Instead, Americans were suddenly confronted with a complicated, horrible reality.

Soon, American soldiers began coming home dead in "body bags." Large numbers of Vietnamese people were killed too. One visitor estimated that for every Vietcong soldier killed in the conflict, two to six Vietnamese civilians also died. Every day, TV announcers reported the day's body count—the number of enemy soldiers killed. Americans at home saw a lot of the war, but it took them a while to understand what they were seeing. Once they did, many Americans—especially college students—began to question if the killing was worth it.

TEACH-INS

To help students become better informed about the war, professors at the University of Michigan in Ann Arbor created a mass educational experience called a "Vietnam teach-in." It was held on March 24, 1965, soon after the first marines landed at Da Nang. The teach-in attracted an audience of 3,000. Students who had been shy in class began challenging professors; positions for and against the war were debated all night.

Weary U.S. soldiers slowly file past fallen comrades in body bags. Americans were confronted with the horrible realities of war when body counts became part of daily television broadcasts.

The teach-in idea spread quickly across the country. Later that spring, a teach-in at the University of California in Berkeley attracted 30,000 people. They sang, talked, and debated for 36 hours. Just as Civil Rights "sit-ins"—protests at segregated businesses—had stopped business as usual in the South, the antiwar teach-ins often brought university business to a standstill.

BASIC TRAINING

Another group who learned quickly about Vietnam was the young men drafted into the army. Basic training taught them the official reasons for the U.S. fight; some new soldiers even learned

A soldier dives for safety as a loaded ammunition truck blows up. Recruits were taught about the war in basic training, but many young men didn't understand what was happening in Vietnam until they experienced it.

Vietnamese. But almost none of them were prepared for exotic Vietnam—what one soldier called "an island resort" with palm trees and warmth year-round. They discovered that its beauty could suddenly turn treacherous. A soldier recalled:

> In the Mekong Delta, in the rice paddies, you'd be walking up to your waist in water and the mud would be past your knees. It was the river silt. . . .There was grass that grew eight feet tall. We called it elephant grass. It . . . was very sharp. If you grabbed at it, it would cut your hand open.

Americans were thrust into constant danger. Enemy soldiers melted into the jungles, were hidden by sympathetic peasants, then returned in surprise attacks. As medic David Ross explained:

> The VC would be the farmer you waved to from the jeep in the day who would be the guy with the gun out looking for you at night. . . . We took more casualties from booby traps than we did from actual combat. . . . How do you fight back against a booby trap? You're just walking along and all of a sudden . . . you don't have a leg.

SPRING RESISTANCE

In the year after Fran Galt returned his draft card, he heard nothing definite. During spring break 1965, he and busloads of other students converged on Washington, D.C., to protest the war in Vietnam. A group called Students for a Democratic Society (SDS) had taken the lead in organizing the protest march.

The march drew over 20,000 people—young and old—to the Washington Monument. Planning to deliver a petition to Congress, the crowd streamed down the mall toward the Capitol, where a wall of police met them. "It seemed that the great mass of people would simply flow on through and over the marble buildings," remembered young historian and activist Staughton Lynd, "that our forward motion was irresistibly strong, and that even had someone been shot or

arrested, nothing could have stopped that crowd from taking posses-
sion of its government."

After the march, SDS withdrew from its role as leader of the antiwar movement. From then on, the Student Mobilization Committee,
known as the "Mobe," would gather many smaller groups together to
plan big marches and demonstrations.

One of these smaller groups was Women Strike for Peace. The organization believed, as member Donna Allen said, "Only women are
going to stop this war." She and the other housewives who made up
the organization didn't deny that many men hated the war. But the
women also saw "too many [men] . . . who also felt warlike, or loved
to fight."

In coffee klatches and through door-to-door and street-corner
leafleting, Women Strike for Peace protested the war, the sale of toy
weapons, and legislators' positions on the war. In July 1965, 10 of
the women traveled to Indonesia to meet with women from the
North Vietnamese army and government. The North Vietnamese
women also wanted peace very much. Returning home, the American
women told how U.S. fragmentation bombs lodged pellets in a vic-
tim's bloodstream that were impossible to remove. The American people were beginning to learn the horrible truth about the war.

WHITE PAPERS

With the antiwar movement quite visible, the Johnson administration
published what was called a "White Paper." In this report, Johnson
argued that North Vietnam was planning to take over South Vietnam
and thus had to be stopped. Though some newspapers and senators
supported the paper, others challenged it.

All along, the president handled opposition to his stance on
Vietnam by "minimizing public awareness and debate," wrote historian Brian VanDeMark. For instance, the president never asked Congress for an official declaration of war. Had he done so, Congress
might have voted against him. He never even called the situation in

Around the nation, the Women Strike for Peace organization worked to end the war through demonstrating and helping the country learn more about what was really happening in Vietnam. Here, a demonstration takes place in Bryant Park, New York.

Vietnam a war; it was a "conflict." In addition, Johnson thought a full-scale war in Vietnam might divert attention from his Civil Rights and antipoverty campaigns at home. So Johnson took small cautious steps, refusing to publicly announce such tactics as air strikes and regular bombings against North Vietnam.

As a result, many ordinary citizens were not aware of the government's actions in Vietnam. Local newspapers didn't report war policy in much depth. The Vietnam protest movement was better informed. But when protesters told the truth about the war, their words seemed exaggerated and crazy to others. This split between protesters and other citizens hurt the peace movement. Until larger segments of the country caught up, protesters were often dismissed as "peaceniks," "hippies," or the "lunatic fringe."

HAWKS

For many Americans, the buildup of troops in Vietnam simply meant that the fighting there would soon be over. After all, how could a small country like North Vietnam withstand the military might of the most powerful nation on earth? The war would last three months at most—that's what many Americans expected.

In the summer of 1965, polling revealed that 47 percent of the nation favored sending more troops to Vietnam, 23 percent were unsure, and 19 percent wanted troop numbers to stay the same. Only 11 percent wanted the United States to pull out.

Many Americans, especially members of veterans groups such as the American Legion and Veterans of Foreign Wars, were outraged that anyone would question the government or refuse to serve in the military. Many veterans, especially those who had served in World War II, thought that opposing the government was immoral and cowardly. They often treated protesters with gross disrespect.

The recruits—often called grunts—who fought in Vietnam were very young: 19 was the average age. "They had been raised on World War II movies, particularly those of John Wayne . . . [that made] war an adventure in which the good guys—our guys—were invincible," wrote Albert Marrin in *America and Vietnam: The Elephant and the Tiger.* Their fathers and mothers, sisters and uncles, had seen the same movies. For many parents, sending a son to fight in Vietnam was sad but glorious, a chance for him to become a man and serve his country. Some young people shared this unquestioning patriotism. Even on college campuses, antiwar protesters were often heckled and counterpicketed by students who supported the government's position on the war.

. . . AND DOVES

Since the age of 13, Tom Rodd had studied *The Conscientious Objector's Handbook.* His passion for protest showed up first at Hotchkiss, a private high school, when he wrote a letter to the *New York Times* asking that kids' rights be taken seriously. He later led student protests against increased bus fares at his Pittsburgh, Pennsylvania, public high school. In the summer of 1963, Rodd was arrested in Georgia for Civil Rights activism. The same summer, he was indicted by a federal grand jury for failure to register for the draft. His prepared statement read in part:

> I am a civil disobedient. That was the term coined by [nineteenth-century writer] Henry David Thoreau. . . . I suppose I could have gone to Canada and not registered at all. But it was because of this duty to our laws and because of this duty to society that has set up these laws that I have turned myself in.

After several months of imprisonment for assessment and observation, Tom Rodd was sentenced to five years in prison or to working with an approved CO group, such as the American Friends Service Committee, a Quaker group that Rodd joined. As another part of his probation, he was forbidden to join any protests.

Then, in November 1965, Norman Morrison set himself on fire under the office window of U.S. Secretary of Defense Robert McNamara. Seconds before he ignited himself in his dramatic protest of the war, Morrison sent his daughter Emily running out of his arms to safety. Morrison's fiery death shocked the many Americans who believed in keeping all antiwar protest peaceful. The action also led Tom Rodd to join a demonstration against the Boeing Corporation, a company that built military helicopters. The American Legion, which counterpicketed across the street, mocked the demonstrators. They carried signs: "Free Matches and Gas for You Peace Creeps."

Since taking part in a demonstration amounted to breaking probation, Tom Rodd, on January 6, 1966, was sentenced to four years in prison. He was one of the first draft resisters to go to prison. In his defense, Rodd said:

> I am forced to stand for the girl child burned to death in Bien Hoa [South Vietnam], for the refugee cold and hungry in a camp on the outskirts of Saigon, for the weary guerrilla fighter, for the Buddhist monk who is now a handful of ashes, for the thousands with no legs, thousands more with no eyes, yes, and even for the U.S. Marines now slowly dying in a Philadelphia hospital. . . . And my word from them to this government is this: Stop this war!

PUTTING PRINCIPLES BEHIND BARS

Under a government which imprisons any unjustly, the true place for a just man is also in prison.

— Henry David Thoreau, "On the Duty of Civil Disobedience," 1847

Civil disobedience was at the heart of Vietnam protest. Nineteenth-century writer Henry David Thoreau had coined the term in his 1847 essay "On the Duty of Civil Disobedience." Thoreau made it clear that by *civil* disobedience he meant peaceful resistance involving civilians, not soldiers.

The twentieth-century Civil Rights movement had modeled its philosophy and many of its tactics—including nonviolent sit-ins, marches, and demonstrations—on Thoreau's ideas. Pacifists began to copy the same tactics. Their reasons included a distaste for violence in any form. In addition, nonviolent action gave the peace activists a "moral edge" over their often violent opponents.

Martin Luther King Jr. also influenced the Vietnam protesters. In his "Letter from Birmingham Jail," King described an unjust law as "a code that a . . . majority group compels a minority group to obey but does not make binding on itself." The document continued, "A law is unjust if it is inflicted on a minority that, as a result of being denied the right to vote, had no part in enacting or devising the law."

King's letter referred to African Americans, who were frequently denied the right to vote in the American South but who were forced to obey laws in which they had no voice. The antiwar protesters could relate to this contradiction. In the 1960s, many young men were drafted into the military at age 18. Yet until 1971, the voting age in most states was 21.

Though King's leadership and writings were powerful influences, Thoreau's writing perhaps meant more to the mainly white antiwar protesters. Thoreau's wit appealed to the young nonconformists. Taking a stand against slavery, for example, Thoreau claimed that any man who cooperated with slavery was no better than a lump of wood:

> The mass of men [who] serve the state . . . [as] standing army, and the militia, jailers, constables put themselves on a level with wood and earth and stones. . . . I know this well, that if . . . one HONEST man, in this State of Massachusetts, ceas[ed] to hold slaves, were actually to withdraw from this copartnership [with the state] and be locked up in the county jail therefore, it would be the abolition of slavery in America.

Thoreau spent a night in jail for refusing to pay taxes to a country that allowed slavery. The experience taught him that "a minority is powerless while it conforms to the majority; . . . but it is irresistible when it clogs by its whole weight." Clogging the machine of American government was exactly what young pacifists and draft resisters were learning to do.

FROM 2-S TO 4-F AND BACK AGAIN

Once President Johnson sent the marines to Vietnam in March 1965, draft calls increased significantly. In September 1965, 27,500 young men were drafted, more than in any other month since the Korean War in the early 1950s. By December 1965, the monthly calls had reached 40,200.

In response, many young men burned their draft cards, the first in 1964. By August 1965, the government saw draft-card burning as such a threat that the action was made a federal offense, punishable by five years in prison. The FBI also kept a close watch on young men who tried to evade the draft by changing addresses, moving to Canada, or "going underground"—disappearing.

Draftees used many other tricks to avoid service. During induction physical exams, some men tried to appear mentally ill—overloading their bodies with caffeine or other drugs and acting unbalanced. Others exaggerated physical defects to make themselves appear unfit for combat.

Men who were enrolled in college didn't need to put on an act. Students usually received 2-S (student) draft deferments: They were exempt from service as long as they kept up their grades and took a full load of college credits. But as Allen Hawley, a British citizen (but an American resident and thus eligible for the draft), discovered in 1970, a 2-S deferment could be revoked when a draft board's patience wore out.

During Hawley's junior year at the University of California in Long Beach, he received a notice to report for induction. Stunned, he visited his draft counselor, who explained that Hawley had neglected to enroll for both summer sessions the previous year and had thus jeopardized his deferment.

Rather than evade the draft by going back to England, Hawley reported for his physical. His bad eyesight earned him an immediate dismissal. Nevertheless, the army tried to induct him a second time, and army doctors only reluctantly admitted that Hawley's poor eyesight made him 4-F—unfit for military service.

WORKING-CLASS WAR

The young men who did *not* resist the draft were often right out of high school, working in factories or on farms. Many were poor men who didn't plan to go to college. Whereas middle-class young men could usually just stay in school to avoid the draft, many poor men had no choice but to serve. Many of these soldiers were black.

In winter 1967, Dr. Martin Luther King Jr. spoke in New York's Riverside Church. He explained how black soldiers—who often didn't have equal rights in their own country—were losing their lives for the rights of others in Vietnam. Blacks were dying "in extraordinarily high proportions," King said, "to guarantee liberties in Southeast Asia that they had not found in Southwest Georgia or East Harlem." King's speech brought attention to the link between racism and the war.

Another Civil Rights worker, John Otis Sumrall, explained in a speech in 1966:

> The local draft board there in Clarke County [Mississippi]. . . . are the same people that are so down on Negroes now. They are especially down on me and some of the people that work with me. They are the same people that beat people while they are trying to demonstrate or exercise their constitutional rights. . . . There are more black people now being inducted in the armed services in the South simply because . . . the white people are afraid of [Civil Rights]. . . . If they can't scare [us]. . . shoot [us]. . . then they use the legal way and draft [us] into the army. . . . I'm going to stay here and fight the real battle for freedom.

Sumrall noted that members of the local draft boards in his state were all white. He brought a lawsuit to prohibit white draft boards from inducting blacks into the military until blacks were equally represented on the boards.

Those blacks who resisted the draft encountered racism as well. When Robert Penn entered Harvard University in Cambridge, Massachusetts, in 1966, he was one of only 21 black men in the class of 1,200. During Penn's first few years at Harvard, he came to see Vietnam as an "unjust war." He thought his father, a minister, would support him in applying for CO status. But his father had different views. Robert explained:

> He said he couldn't support me. When he had served in the military during World War II, the military gave mobility to blacks. Professional black men benefited from the GI bill that paid for their college degrees and give them Veterans Administration mortgages.

Robert had entered Harvard as an optimistic student, seeing the school as a stepping stone to better things. But during his freshman year, he'd been called a "nigger" on campus. He thought about joining SDS, but he wasn't convinced that the mostly white students

A group of hand-holding demonstrators leads a march through New York City in civil protest.

"would understand that things would be different because I was black." He explained, "If I'd gone to a draft-card burning, I'd have been the only one blamed. If you're the only black in the room, you're the one who gets blamed."

THE NEW GENERATION

Around the country, antiwar protests heated up, drawing larger and larger crowds and occurring more and more often. These demonstrations were sometimes spontaneous and illegal—held without a permit—but they were mainly nonviolent.

The largest protest up to that point occurred in Sheep's Meadow in New York's Central Park on April 15, 1967. It attracted a huge cross section of people. Three hundred thousand people—young and old, with long hair and short, housewives and businessmen, nuns and priests, doctors, college professors, and veterans wearing medals—all showed up to register their frustration and outrage. The Student Mobilization Committee, which had organized the demonstration, called for a massive draft-card burning at the event. Though many argued against the action since it was a federal offense, more than 175 young men, including one army reservist, burned their cards in the drizzle.

But the march did not convince the president to scale down the war. Instead the Johnson administration labeled the demonstrators "communists" and accused them of working for the North Vietnamese. The president called those who had burned their draft cards "crazy people" and added that they put the country in grave danger.

Time magazine did not agree. For its 1967 "Man of the Year" issue, *Time* honored the "New Generation" of young activists. In its report, the magazine praised "today's youth [for being] more deeply committed to the fundamental Western ethos—decency, tolerance, brotherhood—than almost any generation since the age of chivalry." *Time,* like many other news sources of the day, noted the "generation gap" that was splitting many young people from their elders.

On October 21, 1967, in Washington, D.C., many from the old generation joined the new generation for one of the largest marches ever held against the war. After listening to speeches and antiwar songs, a small group stormed through a line of soldiers protecting the Pentagon—U.S. military headquarters—and, with thousands following them, camped on the Pentagon lawn. Many stayed until dawn.

"Fully seven hundred people [were] arrested," wrote Kirkpatrick Sales. "At least twice that number had been beaten and bloodied, . . . yet the demonstrators would not give an inch." The Johnson administration scurried to enforce stricter control of the Pentagon grounds, but the lesson could not be erased: "For the first time," wrote Sales, the U.S. "had used its own troops to threaten its own white middle-class children."

FROM DRAFT REFUSER TO CONVICT

One morning in April 1966, Fran Galt opened the door of his campus apartment and saw a U.S. marshal. The marshal had come to deliver Fran's second draft notice in person. The notice told Fran to report for induction. He did not comply.

For refusing induction, Fran was sentenced to four years at the federal prison in Springfield, Missouri. In August he was arrested and placed in a Hennepin County jail in Minnesota to await the journey to Missouri. The marshal who handcuffed Fran was sympathetic. He hoped the war would be over before his own 14-year-old son had to face the draft.

Fran said he "was relieved to have [jail] finally come. I didn't have to wonder anymore." As soon as he was out on bail, he married his girlfriend, Judy. "Once I was in federal prison, we knew it would be easier for Judy to visit if we were married," Fran remembered.

He was 20 years old. Handcuffed to a waist chain, he rode to Missouri in the back of a car driven by two U.S. marshals. His handcuffs and chain made eating difficult. But the marshals weren't concerned—"I was just luggage to them," Fran said.

Inside the "bleak, high, barbed-wire fence" of the prison, he became number 9245. He slept in a dormitory with 125 other men, where the toilets had see-through glass walls and there were no doors on the stalls. He could correspond with only 12 people on an approved list; his letters were censored. He could receive visitors only once a month. When his wife came to visit, they could spend a maximum of two hours in the morning and two hours in the afternoon together, sitting across a coffee table from each other.

For the first 10 months of the 17 months Fran served, there were few other draft resisters in the prison. Then another prison closed, and 50 draft cases from that prison were shipped to Springfield. Most were Jehovah's Witnesses—a group that claimed that all its members were ministers and that all deserved exemptions as religious leaders. Some draft boards accepted this argument, others did not.

In addition to the Jehovah's Witnesses, the draft resisters with Fran included Paul, a member of a small Russian pacifist sect. Paul's family had left Russia so they could be free to practice their beliefs—precisely the same beliefs for which Paul was in prison.

As the months passed, Fran saw himself less as a "draft refuser" and more as a convict. In March 1968, he gained parole. Shortly afterward he wrote, "A few days before my release, I realized that there were emotions, feelings, passions which had been absent in my life for months. . . . [Even now] there is still a deadness which I have been unable to shake off." Fran concluded that his time spent in prison and the dead feeling inside hadn't been worth it. He urged other young men to search for alternative ways to protest the war.

CRAZIES, CANADA, AND THE COLUMBIA REVOLT

When I do get back to the States, I [want to] take the face of American-white-middle-classdom who hold the power... and rub it, without pity, in the blood and gore of what they are doing to the people of the world.

——Conscientious objector
serving in Vietnam

Fran Galt was still in prison during the brutal fighting of early 1968. In other years, fighting had been suspended by both sides during Tet, the Vietnamese new year. But that year, on the morning of January 31—the first day of Tet—an explosion rocked the American embassy in Saigon, South Vietnam. The grim violence that came to be called the Tet Offensive had begun.

Attacks broke out in other cities, villages, and military camps throughout South Vietnam—all of them surprises that the Vietcong and North Vietnamese had been planning for months. They attacked, captured, or executed anyone remotely sympathetic to the Americans. For three weeks, fighting raged, especially in the city of Hue.

In the end, American forces stopped the offensive. But in trying to save themselves, many Americans killed the very people they were supposed to be protecting—the South Vietnamese. Often, in the heat of battle, American soldiers couldn't tell whom they were killing. Other times, to root out the Vietcong, Americans blew up entire neighborhoods, killing thousands of innocent South Vietnamese and leaving many more homeless.

The notion that Americans soldiers cared about protecting South Vietnamese civilians was shot to pieces. The Tet Offensive taught the South Vietnamese, in the words of writer Tobias Wolff, "that for all our talk of partnership and brotherhood we disliked and mistrusted them, and that we would kill every last one of them to save our own skins."

Watching the Tet Offensive on the TV news shocked the American public into new awareness. Because of a new telecommunications satellite, Americans could see the events of the offensive each day as

Crowds gather for a mass funeral service while city officials of Hue, responsible for identifying the victims of the 1968 Tet Offensive, arrange the coffins of the dead.

they happened. Americans saw Saigon's chief of police shoot a Vietcong prisoner in the head. They also saw photographs by *Life* magazine's Douglas Duncan showing American soldiers who had fought at Khe Sanh in South Vietnam. The men were haunted, exhausted, smeared with blood and filth.

Many Americans, including respected TV anchorman Walter Cronkite, realized that there was no end in sight to the fighting. Cronkite reported that "the only rational way out [of the war] . . . will be to negotiate, not as victors but as an honorable people who lived up to their pledge to defend democracy, and did the best they could."

A few weeks earlier, five other American leaders, including Dr. Benjamin Spock and the Reverend William Sloane Coffin from Yale University in New Haven, Connecticut, were indicted by a federal grand jury in Boston, Massachusetts, on the charge of conspiracy "to counsel, aid, and abet young men to violate the draft laws." From different directions, Americans were beginning to converge on the idea that the war in Vietnam was senseless and had to cease.

UNFIT FOR SERVICE

As the brutality and chaos of the fighting came home to American youth, young men called up for the draft tried stranger and stranger ways to fail the induction physical. Many psychologists, ministers, and doctors helped them—claiming the young men were mentally or physically disabled, or spiritually opposed to war. But soon the military became wary of these professionals and their diagnoses, and the tactics got the draft dodgers nowhere.

Michael Ochs finished college in 1966, just as the war was escalating. He did not want to fight in Vietnam, so before his induction physical, he asked a medical student friend to help him. The friend advised him to drink iodine, which supposedly made spots appear on the lungs. In addition, "I ate nothing for three days and drank as much Coke as I could down, which would definitely make me look like a diabetic with a raised sugar count," Michael remembered. The friend gave him some Dexamyls. "I didn't sleep for three days," Michael said. No one could pass a physical in that state. Michael's friend summed up the situation: "Legally," he told Michael, "you'll be dead."

But Michael did pass the physical. When an army psychologist asked him what he thought of the army, Michael told the truth: "I think you're a bunch of criminals—I hope there are war crimes trials. I wish I had the nerve to go over there, 'cause I'd love to work for the other side."

This was no idle threat. Stories of GIs (American soldiers) who had deserted to help the North Vietnamese were circulating at home. The psychologist found Ochs unfit for military service. He couldn't get out of the doctor's office fast enough.

Ochs's case was mild. In their frenzy to avoid serving in Vietnam, men starved themselves for months to get under the required weight, slashed their wrists to look like attempted suicides, zoned out on drugs, and more. One man rolled into a ball on the army psychiatrist's floor and bleated like a goat. Another claimed to be a wizard who could change the weather. Gradually, the military wised up to these tricks and refused to take them seriously.

FROM SOLDIERS TO PACIFISTS

Many GIs eventually joined the resistance movement as well. Seeing so many deaths and fighting a war that never seemed to end wore down the Americans in Vietnam. "I got to the point where I didn't know what I was there for or why," said one. When he was discharged in San Francisco, California, he recalled:

> There was no parade for us. Just a couple of shrinks in white coats, asking, "Did it bother you? Would you like to talk about it?" No, I didn't want to talk about it. I agreed with the antiwar demonstrators. All these kids saying they didn't want to go. I was right behind them. "Right on. Don't go."

Soldiers often went from fighting to helping those in need. Here, a U.S. marine treats the wounds of a young girl who received burns after her village was attacked.

Some men resisted while they were still in the army. Some applied for conscientious objector status and served out their time without again picking up a gun. Sometimes, though, COs were pressured to start shooting and killing again.

Sometimes resistance developed suddenly, taking a soldier by surprise. In one instance, a handful of American soldiers refused to help their friends slaughter Vietnamese people in the village of My Lai, South Vietnam. Though the massacre shocked the American public and the officer in charge was court-martialed, the soldiers who had resisted still felt guilty and had trouble explaining to themselves and others why, all of a sudden, they could not kill.

NORTH OF THE BORDER

Harvey Sachs went through his induction physical pretty sure that he could not serve even as a typist in Vietnam. He was Jewish, born a year after the defeat of Adolf Hitler, the German leader responsible for killing six million Jewish people, as well as millions of others, during World War II. How could Harvey support the systematic killing of ordinary people in Vietnam? He knew that he didn't want to apply for a CO exemption. Nor did he want to go to prison. He wanted to continue to study music. So Harvey and his wife made the difficult decision to emigrate to Canada.

Canada was not involved in the Vietnam War, and its government had made it relatively easy for young Americans to cross the border and escape the draft. The FBI could not arrest U.S. citizens on Canadian soil, and the Canadian government often chose not to extradite U.S. citizens who had fled the draft. Harvey knew, however, that if he left the United States, he might never return or see again people who were important to him. And he worried:

> What to do if the U.S. border guards turned back a young guy headed for Canada with more than a weekend's worth of luggage in tow and a 1-A [fit for service] draft card in his wallet—or if the Canadian immigration authorities didn't grant us Landed Immigrancy?

But neither the U.S. nor Canadian guards bothered Harvey and his wife. In fact, the man who interviewed the couple at the Canadian Department of Manpower and Immigration made their entry easy. He even suggested that they tell other young draft resisters to get an encouraging letter from a Canadian employer.

Harvey and his wife were able to rent a small apartment in Toronto, Ontario, and find work. He sent his new address to his draft board in Ohio, which ordered him by mail to report for induction. FBI agents visited Harvey's relatives and neighbors in Cleveland, urging them to turn him in if he ever returned. Harvey wrote:

> Thereafter, I repeatedly had a nightmare in which I was pursued by armed, expressionless men. . . . I hid in a laundry basket. . . . I would wake up just as I was about to be caught.

The nightmare, along with a tense pain in his jaw, soon went away. "And so, for nearly nine years, did the United States."

Other draft dodgers didn't have such an easy time in Canada. As the war dragged on, many Canadian cities became glutted with American resisters. Canadian companies stopped hiring Americans, and without a job, draft dodgers couldn't stay long. At the border, Canadian officials sometimes grilled American men for hours under bright lights. More and more draft resisters in Canada were immediately put on the next flight back to the United States.

COMING CLEAN FOR THE ELECTION

In early 1968, thousands of college students poured into New Hampshire to set up campaign headquarters for Senator Eugene McCarthy, a presidential candidate from Minnesota who opposed the war in Vietnam. Many young people pinned their hopes for peace on McCarthy, the Democratic Party, and the 1968 presidential election. (The students had no fondness for the Republicans, who supported the war and didn't seem to offer any hope of withdrawal from Vietnam.)

The first test for Senator McCarthy came in a series of primary elections that led up to the national election. In the first primary, held in New Hampshire, McCarthy ran against President Johnson. "Coming Clean for Gene" was the slogan of the students, who cut their hair, shaved their beards, and put on "establishment" clothes to persuade conservative factory workers and housewives to vote for McCarthy's peace ticket. The results were encouraging. In the New Hampshire Democratic primary, McCarthy won 40 percent of the vote.

Shortly after the New Hampshire primary, Senator Robert Kennedy also threw his hat into the Democratic presidential campaign, citing "disastrous, divisive policies" in the country. Kennedy came from a popular political family. His brother was President John F. Kennedy—who had been assassinated in 1963. Many activists thought Robert Kennedy could most effectively unite voters against the war. SDS leader Tom Hayden remembered, "I instinctively liked

Bobby Kennedy. . . . He was the only candidate who could win votes from ghetto blacks and Irish hard hats, the two conflicting poles of a potential populist coalition."

Suddenly, President Johnson was confronted with two opponents within his own party. Johnson's supporters were nervous about his chance for reelection. Some urged a halt to the bombing of North Vietnam to allow peace negotiations to begin. Another group of Johnson's trusted friends and associates, dubbed the "Wise Men" by the press, told the president that the war in Vietnam could not be won and that the United States should get out. They were concerned that the war was dividing the country.

On March 31, the president responded. In a speech, he called a halt to the bombing of North Vietnam and invited North Vietnam to negotiate a peace settlement. At the end of the speech, he added, "I shall not seek, and I will not accept, the nomination of my party for another term as your president."

Johnson's withdrawal was a shock to many. But a bigger shock came on April 4 when Dr. Martin Luther King Jr. was assassinated in Memphis, Tennessee. African Americans were outraged, and riots broke out in black neighborhoods in 125 cities. Washington, D.C., was the hardest hit. Troops ringed the city to maintain order. Soon Congress passed a Civil Rights bill with an antiriot provision. The law made it a federal crime to cross state lines to incite a riot. This law would later be used against antiwar activists.

Despite Johnson's gesture toward peace, he then called up another 24,500 reserve troops for Vietnam, a politically unpopular move. At the same time, the government set a ceiling—no more than 549,000 American troops in Vietnam altogether. Instead of using more Americans to fight, the government started a policy called "Vietnamization." This system turned the ground fighting over to South Vietnamese troops. The United States, meanwhile, would use increased bombing.

Eventually, the U.S. would drop more bombs on Vietnam than all the Allies had used during World War II. To many antiwar activists,

Vietnamization simply meant "a change in the color of the bodies" that died.

STUDENT REVOLT

April also witnessed one of the largest and bloodiest student revolts in the country's history. It began on April 23, 1968, when the SDS chapter at Columbia University in New York called a protest against the university's work for the Institute for Defense Analysis, an arm of the Pentagon. The students also demanded that a new university gym be opened to nearby black residents.

Mark Rudd, leader of the protest and head of the university's SDS chapter, wrote to Columbia president Grayson Kirk: "If we win, we will take control of your world. . . . You call for order and respect for authority; we call for justice, freedom and socialism. . . . I'll use [the words of black activist] Leroi Jones . . . 'Up against the wall—this is a stickup.'"

Students took the acting dean hostage and occupied university buildings. During the week-long occupation, protesters ate food donated by outside sympathizers, sang, argued, and even got married. In the early morning hours of the eighth day, April 30, about 1,000 police entered the buildings and began attacking students and dragging them out. The buildings were cleared, and waves of students and bystanders were stampeded in what historians would later call "a police riot." More than 700 students were arrested; 150 students and faculty were injured.

Classes were canceled for three days, and afterward thousands of students went on strike. They occupied a university building and a university-owned tenement, only to be attacked again by police, who made a number of arrests.

The Columbia revolt signaled a new vision of what students wanted: the right not only to protest university policies but also, as Tom Hayden wrote in *Ramparts* magazine shortly after the strike, "to expand the strike so that the U.S. must either change or send its

Tensions begin to mount at Columbia University in New York, New York, as police prepare to evict protesting students.

troops to occupy American campuses. . . . We are moving toward power—the power to stop the machine [U.S. government] if it cannot be made to serve humane ends."

THE MOVEMENT BEYOND THE MOVEMENT

Girls Say Yes to Boys Who Say No.
— Antiwar slogan

Initially, the most visible antiwar protesters were white male college students—those who were eligible for the draft but who also had the resources and skills to organize against it. They came from mostly middle-class families, often with a history of political involvement. But, throughout the late 1960s, the peace movement broadened to include Americans from more walks of life. War resisters no longer fit the white male stereotype.

Anne Dodge Simpson, for instance, was a product of the proper 1950s middle class. She did what was expected: married, settled in a wealthy Minneapolis, Minnesota, suburb, and had "healthy, rosy-cheeked children and clean floors."

But this secure world blew open for her when, on November 22, 1963, she heard President John F. Kennedy's assassination reported live over her kitchen radio. For the next five years, she took small steps through the door of change. By 1969 she had remarried, resigned from the country club, and gone back to school at the University of Minnesota, where she became involved in antiwar protest.

Her second husband, Bob Simpson, was an associate minister in a suburban church. "I was a token activist," Bob explained. The conservative senior minister supported Bob. But when his boss was out of town, Bob spoke for a more liberal social position and tried to give voice to the minority groups in his church and community.

Soon Bob took a job at Macalester Plymouth Church in St. Paul, Minnesota, next to Macalester College. There he was in the thick of campus protest. He discovered that "about 10 to 15 percent of the student protesters had a position with integrity and meaning. A whole bunch of others were happy to have a chance to raise Cain about something. . . . They were joy riders who liked the excitement but didn't really care, pro or con, about the war."

YOUNG WOMEN ON THE FRONT LINE

"I got high on the righteous indignation of the students," Anne Simpson says of her antiwar activity. "It was wonderful to see this much energy. And I enjoyed rebelling—against my background and upbringing, where it had not been okay to question. Now I enjoyed the freedom to break some of the rules."

Yet women in the antiwar movement were often seen as second-tier activists. A popular antiwar slogan, "Girls Say Yes to Boys Who Say No," underscored the feeling of many that women were important to the movement only as supportive girlfriends and wives of the draft resisters.

Jim Moore recalled a definite gender split in the antiwar community. "Women were supportive of my antiwar effort," Jim said, "but men had to deal with the war—they had a bond. Women did a lot of the nitty-gritty work of protest; men did a lot of the [showy] stuff."

The difference had to do with the draft, Jim believed. Women might choose to serve as nurses in Vietnam, but they did not have to worry about being drafted. Debbie Notkin, who counseled young men on draft resistance, agreed. "I think most of the women . . . including myself, were doing it partly out of a sense of guilt that we weren't at the same kind of risk as our male friends."

Some women did serve in the military as nurses. But few American nurses—or doctors, for that matter—were prepared for the medical disasters they faced in Vietnam: strange diseases, painful wounds caused by fragmentation bombs that peppered the skin, and exposure to Agent Orange—a highly toxic chemical used to defoliate trees that also led to skin rash, fatigue, dizziness, and cancer long after veterans returned home.

It was hard to write home to what one nurse called "the peaceful side of the planet." Shortly after nurse Winnie Smith returned to the

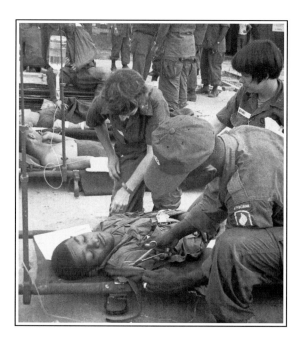

U.S. army doctors and nurses tend to wounded paratroopers at a field hospital.

United States in 1967, she was asked to appear on TV. The reporter asked her what kinds of wounds she had seen in Vietnam. As she remembers, she "shut down the part of me that want[ed] to cry how awful it was. The interviewer would think it too political. Families might not be ready to hear it. . . . I [told him I] saw gunshot wounds, burn wounds, head wounds, blast wounds. I [didn't] say bellies full of pus, or crispy critters, or blown-off arms and legs, or fixed and dilated pupils left to die alone."

Even though she was relieved to be home, Winnie couldn't join her stateside friends in holiday parties nor sympathize with coworkers who complained about long hours and difficult medical cases. Although bothered by some of the antiwar protest—students burning the American flag and Vietnam vets throwing away their medals—she knew that she had to take part.

NO RECOVERY, NO R&R

As a high school student, Lisa Boehlke lived in Singapore with her missionary family in the late 1960s. There, she and her friends became the confidantes of American servicemen sent to Singapore for Rest and Recreation (R&R). She remembered:

> They were scared in a way I haven't seen anyone since. "I'm so glad to speak English," they would say. "You remind me of my sister or cousin." These were not come-on lines. (The guys in the antiwar movement had much more creative come-on lines.) The GIs spoke with sorrow in their voices. . . . They were confused. They thought they were there to fight the war for the Vietnamese but sometimes they worked harder than the South Vietnamese soldiers over the ridge.

A marine officer told her how his men had fought two months to take one hill. They had had difficulty getting supplies and maintaining radio contact. Eventually, most of the men were killed. And three days after the company had succeeded, they were told by the general's office to abandon the hill. "These were my men," agonized the marine. "I led my men into combat just so they could get killed."

Another soldier mourned that he had been unable to save a wounded buddy. "They radioed for a helicopter to come in right away and take out the wounded," he told Lisa, "but the guys at the field yelled back over the wires, 'This copter's scheduled for the [food] run.'" His friend died before the medics arrived.

"We were too young to be counseling these young men," Lisa remembered. "But we listened. Even then I realized that they did not connect their confusion and anger against the war with taking a political position against it." But Lisa did. When she and her family returned to the United States in 1970, she went to college and immediately became active in antiwar protests.

"1, 2, 3, 4, WE WILL FIGHT YOUR WAR NO MORE!"

Sue Lommen left a convent in central Minnesota feeling "ripped off, lied to, screwed over, and pissed off." Some of her anger came from messages of the Civil Rights and antiwar movements that had trickled slowly into her all-white, working-class town. A few years after she left the convent, she was married and pregnant and involved in protest work, writing letters and making phone calls. She tried joining a demonstration, but her husband made it clear that "he didn't want me running around in public pregnant."

Sue backed off, but she soon became involved in the Catholic Newman Center at Mankato State University in Minnesota, where her husband was going to school. At the Newman Center, nuns spoke about their work with poor people in Central America. These discussions helped Sue connect social activism with her religious background. Finally, in the early 1970s, she moved to Minneapolis and separated from her husband.

Soon after Sue was settled, she went to a military funeral at Fort Snelling in Minneapolis—one of her cousins had come home from Vietnam in a body bag. "He was a shy person," she remembered, "an

The strain of battle shows on the faces of these soldiers.

angelic person. He would do anything for anyone. . . . We had heard about My Lai [the massacre in the South Vietnamese village]. Mike would never have done that. He would probably have protected old Vietnamese women and children and gotten killed in the process." Perhaps that had happened; Sue's family never knew the circumstances of her cousin's death. After his funeral she recalled:

> I felt the need to act. I began marching against the war. I felt good walking . . . seeing people who were really different from me, people from other cultures. I felt I was finally part of a bigger world. I took my freedom. Every step creating positive energy toward peace. We sang "Kum-ba-ya," Civil Rights songs with new words. We'd be in front of the Federal Building. "One, two, three, four, we will fight your war no more." We'd yell until we were hoarse, hoping somebody would hear.

NIGHTSTICK CITY

In late April 1968, Vice President Hubert Humphrey became the third Democrat to announce his candidacy for the presidency. Calling for a "politics of happiness . . . of purpose . . . of joy," Humphrey didn't appeal to the antiwar protesters—who saw little in national politics to make them happy. Many activists backed Eugene McCarthy. Others supported Robert Kennedy.

Then, on June 7, 1968, Kennedy was assassinated after winning the California primary. With his slaying, many young people became disillusioned with the political process. They began to doubt that normal politics and voting in elections could stop the war.

The week after Kennedy's assassination, Students for a Democratic Society held its annual national convention at Michigan State University in East Lansing. Some members hoped to plan a protest for the upcoming Democratic National Convention in Chicago, Illinois. But the meeting turned ugly instead.

Some SDS members wanted their group to embrace communism—which was then in place in the Soviet Union, China, and other nations. The convention hall boasted pictures of Soviet leaders Vladimir Lenin and Leon Trotsky, the Soviet hammer and sickle, the flags of communism and anarchism, and copies of Chinese Chairman Mao Zedong's *Little Red Book* of sayings.

But this display was mild compared to the bickering among factions. One group, led by Bernadine Dohrn, wanted to turn SDS into a revolutionary organization of students and the poor. Another faction, the Progressive Labor Party (PL), opposed Dohrn's ideas and managed to have them defeated.

The convention then deteriorated into an attack on the PL. "PL Out! PL Out!," members shouted. But the PL stayed, and the convention did nothing to decide what kind of protest should be mounted at the Democratic Convention scheduled for August.

A WAR IN THE STREETS

The Mobe did have a strategy for the convention, however. Setting up an office in Chicago, SDS veterans Rennie Davis and Tom Hayden wanted to create "sustained, organized protests" at the convention. But they and other members of the Mobe were afraid that mobs of angry demonstrators would clog the streets and attack convention delegates.

Then the funky Youth International Party, or "Yippies," joined in the planning—and the chance for solid, effective demonstrations looked even bleaker. The Yippie plan for a "Festival of Life" sounded like a formula for random nonsense and petty violence: a pig candidate for president, slashed tires, nude bathing in the lake, prostitutes, and 100,000 burned draft cards. Plans were complicated further by the Chicago police and Mayor Richard Daley's refusal to issue permits for antiwar marches or gatherings.

The Yippies threatened to slip drugs into the city's water system and to bombard the convention with mortars. Mayor Daley didn't want to take any chances. He put the police and National Guard on alert and had the convention hall ringed with barbed wire and barricades. "The Convention thus became, even before it convened, the first national convention in memory to require the protection of troops," wrote the *New York Times*.

The last week in August, a motley array of 5,000 protesters—from groups as diverse as Clergy and Laymen Concerned about the War, Women Strike for Peace, and the Communist Party—began to arrive in Chicago. Five thousand was far fewer people than organizers had anticipated, but numbers grew throughout the week.

On Saturday August 24, in Lincoln Park and the surrounding streets, the action began peaceably, with bongo drumming and guitar music. But as the protest progressed into Sunday and then into Monday, the fuses of protesters and police burned shorter. Poet Allan Ginsberg sang a meditation chant—*Om . . . om . . . om . . . om*—to try and quiet the crowd. Then a truck full of Yippies pulled into the park; the truck became a rallying point for protesters shouting: "Kill the Pigs [police]."

For several hours, the police stood still for the taunts and burning cigarettes thrown at them. But they eventually charged with their nightsticks, beating anyone within reach. Many officers removed their badges to avoid detection. Many shouted, "Kill the Commies." Even reporters and photographers were beaten.

Surging through streets, the protesters chanted "Ho, Ho, Ho Chi Minh" and held aloft a Vietcong flag. "Hell no, we won't go," shouted the crowd when a police megaphone blared a curfew. The rallying cry of draft refusers was being used to resist the police force at home.

The Mobe did have one permit, for a rally at the Grant Park band shell on Wednesday, August 28. Tuesday, a police superintendent said

Police arrest a protester as a rally at Grant Park in Chicago, Illinois, in 1968 becomes violent.

he'd allow a crowd to stay in the park overnight if they were peaceful. While the crowd listened to the folk group Peter, Paul, and Mary sing *This Land Is Your Land* and *If I Had a Hammer,* the police brought in the National Guard, armed with M-1 rifles, carbines, shotguns, ammunition, and gas masks. The crowd yelled obscenities, but the guardsmen held their calm.

Finally, Wednesday afternoon, 10,000 people arrived at Grant Park for the scheduled Mobe rally. Police handed out flyers reminding the crowd that they had no permission to march to the amphitheater, site of the Democratic Convention.

Some demonstrators wanted the American flag flown at half-mast—"as a symbol that democracy at the Democratic Convention was dead." When a youth shinnied up the flagpole and began to lower the flag, an argument rippled through the crowd. About 20 police officers charged into the throng, and demonstrators began throwing "anything they could get their hands on," said one observer, "heavy chunks of concrete, sticks, cans, bags of what looked like

Police and demonstrators clash outside the 1968 Democratic National Convention in Chicago.

paint." Eventually, the demonstrators would add flaming rags, shoes, and even bags of excrement to their arsenal.

The police force increased to 50, regrouped, and plowed into the crowd, nightsticks raised, helmet visors down. Mobe marshals could not contain the demonstrators. A red flag was run up the flagpole; the police managed to get it down. Finally, the police attacked, "flailing with their clubs in all directions."

Nora Sayre, who reported on the event, wrote, "I saw seven policemen beating one girl—long after she had fallen; a row of sitting singers whose heads were cracked open by a charge of running cops." A medic in a white coat with a Red Cross armband was beaten to the ground by the police.

Thirty police were also injured, and an untold number of demonstrators lay bleeding and crying for help. As the crowd straggled back together, the Mobe announced a march to the amphitheater. The demonstrators sat down to wait while Mobe leaders tried to negotiate a march path with the police. Finally, as the glare of TV cameras became noticeable in the dusk, the demonstrators left the park and ran toward Michigan Avenue. Soon they merged with the Poor People's Campaign, a group lobbying for "Jobs and Food for All."

The police would not let them pass down Michigan Avenue; the crowd was trapped. As a group of demonstrators tried to move down Balbo Street, they met a busload of police. Witnesses heard the police shout, "Kill, Kill, Kill!" Then a police riot erupted, with TV cameras recording it all. "The whole world is watching," cried people in the crowd. Police beat demonstrators who lay on the ground. The deputy superintendent of police tried to pull off his men.

Finally, the pressure of the battle broke the plate-glass window at the front of the Hilton Hotel, and bleeding demonstrators fell into the lounge, followed by the police. On televisions around the United States, citizens witnessed the horror of the street battle between protesters and police.

Inside the convention hall, Hubert Humphrey had just been nominated and Senator Abraham Ribicoff of Connecticut was delivering a nomination speech for Senator George McGovern of South Dakota when TV monitors began showing pictures of the street fighting outside. "With George McGovern, we wouldn't have Gestapo tactics on the streets of Chicago," cried the horrified Ribicoff. The convention broke into bedlam. A motion to adjourn was made, but the convention voted to continue.

Outside, demonstrators who had not fled or been injured or arrested returned to Grant Park. In the convention hall, state-by-state balloting began, and the crowd in the park followed the proceedings by listening to transistor radios. In the eerie shadows of the TV lights, National Guardsmen arrived with machine guns mounted on trucks and placed themselves between the crowd and the Hilton.

When Hubert Humphrey was declared the Democratic candidate for president, many in Grant Park shouted, "No, No!" Humphrey had entered none of the Democratic primaries; many felt his candidacy was a breach of the party system.

Defeated but not beaten, Eugene McCarthy's delegates decided to march in candlelight down Michigan Avenue. The file of flickering lights created a mesmerizing quiet. Police let the marchers pass; demonstrators in Grant Park cheered them.

The next day, another violent battle occurred between police and demonstrators. Several hundred demonstrators were arrested. Then, at 5 A.M. Friday morning, police were called to clear a crowded corridor at the Hilton. They moved into rooms, beating the people there. In his memoir, *The Year of the People,* Eugene McCarthy called the action an unprecedented invasion of privacy.

In the weeklong battles, 700 civilians and 83 police officers were injured, 653 people were jailed, and 65 reporters and photographers were injured, arrested, or had their equipment smashed. What did all this violence mean? For the bulk of the American population, the violence of "Nightstick City" brought home a simple reality: Antiwar demonstration had itself become a war. Many Americans who might have added their voices to peaceful protest were too shocked and frightened to do so.

Other Americans recalled the way southern police had beaten Civil Rights demonstrators earlier in the decade. Many had ignored the beatings when the victims were black. But the fact that the victims were white students in a northern city made people pay attention. The war was beginning to hit home for white America.

The Democratic Party left the Chicago convention with two strikes against it. Its candidate, Vice President Hubert Humphrey—"the Happy Warrior"—would not separate himself from President Johnson's war policy. The party was also "guilty by association" with the "peacenik" street battle.

Richard Nixon strikes a famous pose as he is elected president of the United States in 1968. His wife, Pat, is to his right. Daughters Julie and Tricia stand at Nixon's left. At the far left is David Eisenhower, Julie's fiancé.

Humphrey was not expected to win the election. Many antiwar protesters who would have voted for many other Democratic candidates voted against Humphrey. In the national election in November, the Republican candidate, Richard Nixon, became the next president of the United States.

VIOLENCE AND VIGILS

One side's right, one side's wrong!
We're on the side of the Vietcong!
　　　　　　—Antiwar chant

Richard Nixon had a "secret plan" to end the war in Vietnam. For many years, the North Vietnamese had been sending troops and supplies down the Ho Chi Minh Trail between Vietnam and the neighboring nation of Cambodia. In Cambodia, the Vietcong and North Vietnamese had set up supply bases, hospitals, and refuge centers for their armies.

General Creighton Abrams, who had replaced General Westmoreland as the American commander in Vietnam, convinced President

Nixon that bombing the supply line in Cambodia was necessary to winning the war. In March 1969, Nixon ordered bombings of Cambodia. But, afraid of public reaction at home, he decided to keep the bombings a secret. Thus Nixon began war against Cambodia without following the correct legal process—without asking Congress to declare war first.

SECRETS AND SPIES

For the antiwar protesters, the president had another secret plan. President Nixon called dissenters "young criminals posturing as romantic revolutionaries" and "a severe internal security threat" to the United States. He thus felt justified in spying on them.

The spying took many forms. FBI agents tapped phone wires, infiltrated protest organizations, and disrupted antiwar meetings. Often, spies harassed nonactivist groups, such as bus companies hired to transport people to antiwar protests. One FBI agent recalled: "We might be asked for the names of the 10 most active radical groups in an area. If there were only 4 active groups, we'd have to come up with the names of 6 others. We didn't make any distinction as to whether they were engaged in legal or illegal activities."

Sometimes, the results were ridiculous. The night before Nixon's inauguration, an undercover agent slept beside the Yippie "candidate for president"—Pigasus the pig. Finally, the domestic spy game grew so huge and misguided that Congress called for an investigation.

TRIALS AND LEGALITIES

On March 26, 1971, *Life* magazine published an article about the Senate hearings on government spying. In Minneapolis, Fran and Lester Galt, along with 16 others who were being watched, agreed to pose for the magazine. "We interviewed the *Life* photographers," remembers Fran Galt. "We wanted to know what the FBI had on us. It turned out that the surveillance was just one big clipping service, tracking those who protested publicly and thus got their names in the paper. I didn't think the FBI had to worry about us: We were hardly the ones who'd be planting bombs!"

Four professors at the University of Minnesota were among those photographed, as was Dave Gutknecht, a man who had appealed his conviction for draft resistance all the way to the Supreme Court. Dave argued that his draft board had moved him to the top of the draft list to punish his protest activity. The Supreme Court ruled in Gutknecht's favor, calling the draft board's actions unlawful. The decision opened the way for other imprisoned draft resisters, including Jim Moore, to appeal their convictions and go free.

As the war dragged on, the number of soldiers and civilians who took their cases against the war to court increased. The majority of Supreme Court judges declined to hear one case that nonetheless had a legal impact because two judges, William O. Douglas and Potter Stewart, wrote minority opinions on the case in November 1967. In their opinions, the judges raised important questions about the constitutionality of U.S. involvement in Vietnam. They raised these points:

1. Is the military action in Vietnam truly a "war" as defined by the Constitution?
2. If so, can the president force people to fight even though Congress has not officially declared war?
3. How do the treaties signed by the U.S. in regard to Southeast Asia affect the action in Vietnam?
4. Has the Gulf of Tonkin Resolution of August 10, 1964, covered the military actions that have come since then, and was the Resolution a declaration of war, as defined by the Constitution?

Just as the Supreme Court was beginning to take the antiwar protesters seriously, the president and the secret spying agencies of the government were also taking antiwar activists to court in increased numbers. Many of the trials became known by the place and number of people involved: the Baltimore 4, the Boston 5, the Milwaukee 14, the Chicago 8—which later became the Chicago 7—and the Catonsville 9.

The trial of the Catonsville 9 was one of the more unusual and flamboyant cases. In May 1968, a group of radical Catholics had entered the local draft board in Catonsville, Maryland. They had lugged out 378 files of men classified 1-A and burned the files in a parking lot across the street.

Two among the nine, the brothers and priests Philip and Daniel Berrigan, caught the attention of the nation. Tall and good-looking, Philip Berrigan was, in the words of biographer Francine de Plessix Gray, "the Gary Cooper of the Church." Daniel, a poet, gained

Father Philip Berrigan, **left,** *and his brother, Father Daniel Berrigan,* **right,** *were arrested along with seven others for removing draft board records from the Catonsville, Maryland, draft board office. Here, they watch the records burn.*

attention for the power of his words. In the brothers' lengthy defense, each spoke of religious experiences that had led him to believe the war was immoral.

As the jury deliberated, Judge Roszel C. Thomsen and the defendants discussed their mutual hatred for the war. The judge admired the protesters' principles but insisted that those who broke a law must pay the penalty. Members of the Catonsville 9 received sentences ranging from two to three years.

Despite the long sentences, many other protesters followed the example of the Catonsville 9. Nine other groups destroyed draft records in 1969, including one all-female group. Such violence disturbed many who loved pacifism above all else. Thomas Merton, a Trappist monk and friend of the Berrigans, wrote, "The Peace Movement may be escalating beyond peaceful protest. In which case it may also be escalating into self-contradiction."

THE WEATHERMEN

Contradiction also described Students for a Democratic Society at this time. At SDS's next annual convention, in June 1969, Bernadine Dohrn tried again to lead the group into her revolutionary youth group. This time, her backers had prepared a paper called "You Don't Need a Weatherman to Know Which Way the Wind Blows," a title taken from Bob Dylan's song "Subterranean Homesick Blues."

Dohrn said she wanted to lead SDS away from the "weather" of national politics and instead ally it with the Black Panthers, a radical group that preached black power and separatism from white society. The panthers believed that black men should be exempt from the draft because Vietnam was a "racist war." They also believed in revolutionary violence.

Dohrn tried, as she had the year before, to get the Progressive Labor Party out of SDS. "We are not a caucus," she said of her own faction. "We *are* SDS." Then she stormed out of the hall. SDS member Jared Israel remembered:

> Everybody, including the leaders, was frozen. . . . They were in tears. That's what the reaction was . . . stunned horror, because we saw [Dohrn's group] destroying the organization. We looked around and we saw potheads and crazies and maniacal panthers—we're talking about sickies.

After Dohrn and her group left, SDS tried to regroup, but Jared Israel was right: SDS had lost its power to influence the antiwar movement or other campus political agendas. Dohrn went on to create a new organization called the Weathermen. Members spread in small units around the United States, living in communes and trying to recruit high school students and workers. The Weathermen wanted to "get out of their white skins" and remake themselves. Trying to "liberate" schools, they sometimes barged into classrooms and lectured students and teachers about fascism, racism, imperialism, and "offing the pigs" (killing police). These tactics were rarely successful; many students chased them out of their neighborhoods.

Dohrn was determined, however, to assert her radical vision. She declared October 8–11, 1969, "Days of Rage" in Chicago. Only 400 to 600 students showed up, but that didn't stop Dohrn from leading them in a frenzied attack on downtown Chicago before they were brought under control by police. After that, the Weathermen went underground. They would be responsible for several bombings, one of which killed three of their own members.

Although the Weathermen fought the government, both the Weathermen and the Black Panthers shared a concept with President Nixon—the idea that violence could lead to peace. President Nixon had convinced himself that he could bring an end to the war in Vietnam only by increasing the bloodshed. At the same time, Black Panther Huey Newton preached, "In order to get rid of the gun it is necessary to pick up the gun."

For a while, it seemed that the nation as a whole had turned toward violence. According to one survey, 292 protests had taken place on 232 college campuses during the first six months of 1969. In addition, bombing or other destruction of property had occurred in 24 percent of the protests.

MORATORIUM PLANNING

In April 1969, John Erlichman of Nixon's staff told student leaders, "If you continue to think you can break laws just because you don't agree with them, you're going to force us to up the ante to the point where we have to give out death sentences for traffic violations."

The leaders of some 250 student organizations who had come to Washington, D.C., to confer with the president were stunned by this statement. They told the press, "Nixon is not going to stop the war . . . and it's clear that we have to resume our efforts to stop the war."

From this meeting was born the idea for a nationwide Vietnam Moratorium Day—planned for October 15, 1969. A moratorium is a delay or suspension. As protester David McReynolds later explained:

> The idea was simply to pause, to hold vigils, to gather quietly in town squares, to have meetings on campuses. . . . It was not a general strike, massive legal rally, or a "call to conscience to fill the jails." Quiet, massive, and with politics left vague, it gave every American a chance to be heard. The majority of Americans who did not support Nixon . . . did not want to go to Washington . . . but they were willing to go into town streets with candles. Several million Americans all over the country took part.

The leaders of the moratorium—David Hawk and Sam Brown—counted on a nationwide network of student organizations to make the moratorium a reality. The two rented an office in Washington and took the idea to the Mobe, which agreed to join the project.

Organizing such a huge event cost money—for phones, mailings, and supplies. Donations came in the form of individual $5 and $10 contributions. Many students and adults volunteered their time, and three full-page ads ran in the *New York Times* requesting money. One ad showed a father in a business suit with his arm around his long-

Vietnam Moratorium Day united generations in the common goal of stopping the war.

haired hippie son. The caption read: "October 15, Fathers and Sons Together against the War."

Many people in both generations were united to stop the war. Many members of congress endorsed the moratorium, as did several large labor unions. How could the government fail to notice this huge, peaceful demonstration?

"A NEON OVEN"

While moratorium planning was under way, the trial of the Chicago 8 began in September 1969. The eight defendants were charged with conspiring to cross state lines with the intent of causing a riot at the Democratic Convention in 1968. The eight were Yippie leaders Abbie Hoffman and Jerry Rubin; SDS founders Tom Hayden and Rennie Davis; Black Panther Bobby Seale; pacifist David Dellinger; and John Froines and Lee Weiner, two teachers charged with teaching about the use of bombs.

Judge Julius Hoffman soon showed his bias against the eight. "The substance of the crime," the judge said, "was [the defendants'] state of mind." In turn, the Chicago 8 were far from model defendants. Bobby Seale, after being refused a request to defend himself, called the judge a pig and a fascist. On October 15, the day of the moratorium, the defendants had the tables in the courtroom draped with flags of the United States and the National Liberation Front (NLF)—North Vietnam's army. David Dellinger tried to read the names of dead from both sides of the conflict.

The judge retaliated with charges of contempt of court and eventually had Bobby Seale chained in his chair and gagged so tightly that he often had trouble breathing. It was difficult to proceed with Seale "sitting in a high chair with his wrists and ankles strapped under clanking chains. Wrapped around his mouth and back of his head was a thick white cloth. His eyes and the veins in his neck and temples were bulging with the strain of maintaining his breath," wrote Tom Hayden.

The press covered the trial extensively, and many Americans saw the image of chained Bobby Seale—looking not much different than a chained slave. Several times, when the other defendants protested Seale's treatment, a shouting match ensued among lawyers, defendants, and the judge. "You might as well kill him if you are going to gag him," Abbie Hoffman cried. When the judge told Hoffman that he had no right to address the court, Hoffman retorted, "This, man, isn't a court; this is a neon oven." The court of public opinion was the defendants' main hope. Despite their rage over the treatment of Seale, they were glad to have a national arena for displaying the government's oppression.

As for the charges themselves, none of the eight defendants had gone to Chicago to start a riot. But the judge refused to admit as evidence their many applications to the city for permits to demonstrate and march or their written plan emphasizing that the demonstration should be "nonviolent and legal."

Bobby Seale was eventually unchained and ungagged, and his trial was separated from the group, which then became the Chicago 7.

Though the jury dismissed the conspiracy charge, it found Dellinger, Hayden, Davis, Hoffman, and Rubin guilty of inciting to riot. Judge Hoffman also sentenced all the defendents to various lengths of time in jail for contempt of court—from David Dellinger's two years, five months, and 16 days to Lee Weiner's two months. The judge also denied the defendants bail.

In response, outraged demonstrators took to the streets in Chicago, Washington, Boston, and other cities. An appeals court eventually overturned the sentences, ruling that Judge Hoffman's behavior in the case had been unbefitting a judge.

MORATORIUM ARRIVES

Vietnam Moratorium Day was indeed celebrated nationwide. Some businesses, including Midas Muffler and the Itek Corporation, urged employees to take time off to observe the moratorium. The New York cast of *Fiddler on the Roof* skipped its performance to join the observance.

The largest gathering was in Boston, with 100,000 in attendance. In small towns and big cities, people listened to the reciting of the names of Vietnam dead, gave speeches, and circulated petitions against the war. Some groups held silent candlelight vigils, church services, or processions. No violence jarred the calm certainty of the national show of strength against the war.

But not everyone supported the action. The American Legion urged people to fly the American flag on Vietnam Moratorium Day. In South Dakota, supporters of the war threw "America—Love It or Leave It" leaflets at a moratorium vigil. Countless employees were reprimanded—some were even fired—for participating in the event. And, after the North Vietnamese broadcast a message of support for the moratorium, Vice President Spiro Agnew denounced the event as "consorting with the enemy."

A VIOLENT WAY TO PEACE

The nation has been "driven to use the weapons of war upon its youth."
—President's Commission on Campus Unrest

President Nixon made a speech on November 3, 1969, that hit antiwar demonstrators hard. He said that the protesters threatened the nation's "future as a free society." The enemy was at home, said the president, "North Vietnam cannot defeat or humiliate the United States. Only Americans can do that."

Nixon called on the "great silent majority" to support him. Forty thousand Americans sent in letters doing just that. But many others, especially students, decided to come to Washington to prove the president wrong. They were not trying to defeat or humiliate the United States; they were trying to save it from the ugliness of war.

Nixon's speech cemented the unsteady alliance among the different antiwar groups. Some student groups thought they could create change through the electoral process. Many from the Mobe thought the country was ready for revolution. Whatever their views, protesters joined together for a mid-November mobilization in Washington, D.C.

The mobilization began on November 13 with a "March against Death." Each hour for two and a half days, people carried placards and lighted candles across the Arlington Memorial Bridge, then stopped in front of the White House and called out the names of the many Americans killed in Vietnam. From the White House, they marched to the Capitol and placed the placards in 40 coffins. In the cold and rain, thousands marched with flickering candles and lonely voices, singing out the names of the fallen. It was a haunting pageant, as if the dead had come back to condemn the nation for its earlier indifference.

The morning of November 15 dawned clear and cold. The Mobe's request for permits for a march that day had been granted with reluctance by the government, which greatly exaggerated the potential for violence. The president called in 9,000 troops. Mobe organizers, also worried about violence, used walkie-talkies to stay in contact with the police throughout the day.

Thousands of marchers began to assemble for a walk down Pennsylvania Avenue to the Washington Monument. All told, between 500,000 and 800,000 people attended—the largest political march in the country's history until that time. Yet the government insisted that no TV network would cover the march live. Only short taped scenes would be relayed on the evening news.

The president pretended to carry on business as usual. He reportedly watched a football game on TV. But outside on the streets of Washington, the march began behind three drummers and a line of people carrying coffins with placards listing the Vietnam dead. Marchers smiled at police, flashed peace signs, and chanted slogans. "Ho, Ho, Ho Chi Minh, NLF Gonna Win," "One, Two, Three, Four, Tricky Dick [Nixon] Stop the War," and "Give Peace a Chance" were all called out with good humor. By midday, half a million people waited around the Washington Monument.

Inside the government buildings, few looked out. But one who did was National Security Council aide William Watts, who saw his wife and children filing past the window. The sight upset him. He knew that even a march this big would not change war policy very much.

Later in the day, following Dave Dellinger, many demonstrators broke away toward the Justice Department building. A huge papier-mâché mask of Attorney General John Mitchell was carried aloft. Protesters broke windows and threw bottles at the police, who then let fly the tear gas. The demonstrators filled downtown streets, and small gangs of youths did minor damage. To Mitchell, watching from the fifth floor of the Justice Department, the scene "looked like the Russian Revolution."

When the mobilization was over, the administration tried to downplay its size and exaggerate its violence. The *Washington Post* would have none of this characterization. It wrote on November 18, 1969:

> The effort by this administration to characterize the weekend demonstration as (a) small, (b) violent, and (c) treacherous will not succeed because it is demonstrably untrue. . . . The Nixon administration was less interested in trying to keep the march peaceful than in trying to make it seem less large and more violent than it really was, and in trying to scare the daylights out of the . . . Silent Majority at the same time.

In some ways, President Nixon responded positively—reviving the concept of Vietnamization, scheduling regular withdrawals of American troops from Vietnam, and eventually starting peace talks with North Vietnam. At the same time, however, the administration stepped up its secret and unauthorized missions in Southeast Asia.

On April 30, 1970, Nixon made a televised speech to announce that American and South Vietnamese troops would invade Cambodia. He was convinced that the invasion was necessary to win or end the war. But members of his cabinet warned him that the action would ignite campuses. Aides of Secretary of State Henry Kissinger resigned in protest. Even conservative radio commentator Paul

Harvey told his "middle-America" audience: "America's 6 percent section of the planet's mothers cannot bear enough boy babies to police Asia—and our nation can't bleed to death trying."

Yet Nixon and Kissinger went ahead. In his speech, Nixon said that he had discussed the move with Congress, but that was not true. Senator William Fulbright, chairman of the Senate Foreign Affairs Committee, was so irate that he led Congress to revoke the 1964 Tonkin Gulf Resolution, which had originally allowed President Johnson to send troops to Vietnam.

KENT STATE LIGHTS THE FUSE

Student outrage also exploded—from protests the night after the announcement to violent confrontations over the next weekend. University of Maryland students attacked their Reserve Officer Training Corps (ROTC) center and local police. The National Student Association and leaders of the Vietnam Moratorium Day called for nationwide student strikes, and over 80 percent of the nation's college campuses declared some kind of strike during the last few weeks of spring term.

At Kent State University in Ohio, students set fire to their ROTC building and sliced the hoses of firefighters who tried to put out the fire. As one student said, "Burning down the building was a reasonable answer to an administration that doesn't listen to its students."

In response, Ohio governor James Rhodes called the students "the communist element" and sent 300 National Guardsmen to campus. The students were shocked to see armored personnel carriers, army trucks, and jeeps with guns arrive. The guardsmen were armed with tear gas and M-1 rifles, which they were ordered to put in a "lock and load" position. One general ordered, "Shoot any rioter who cuts a fire hose."

On May 3, hundreds of Kent State students gathered to protest the war and the presence of the National Guard on campus. When the students refused to disperse, the guardsmen sprayed them with tear gas and chased them into town, where they sat down in the street. The guardsmen attacked again, this time with bayonets, and injured several students. As the students fled back to campus, the guardsmen pursued. Tear gas blew into dormitories, sending choking students outside, where they were chased back in by the guardsmen.

The next day, May 4, another demonstration was called for noon. Again students and the National Guard confronted each other. Tear gas canisters were lobbed back and forth. From the students came yells and taunts, bottles and bricks. The guardsmen, young themselves, had been up many hours. They had little experience withstanding the abuse of a crowd. Yet the students did not do them real damage; the closest students stood 23 to 85 yards away.

Suddenly, shots rang out. No one knew if an order to fire had been given. But fire the guardsmen did, into the throng of demonstrating students. Four were killed and nine wounded.

The nation was in shock. A computer printout of schools that either shut down entirely or went on strike after the killing ran 10 feet long. Thirty ROTC buildings were attacked on other campuses during the week, and the National Guard was called to 21 campuses.

The variety of protest was staggering—teach-ins, rallies, workshops, marches, blockades, sit-ins, flag-lowerings, draft-card turn-ins, symbolic funerals. Many students protested for the first time. On Saturday, May 9, a crowd of 130,000, mostly students, gathered in Washington, D.C., to pay somber tribute to their peers at Kent State.

Many older Americans had little sympathy for the dead students. Student activism struck many—especially working-class Americans—as a luxury exercised by spoiled brats. In a *Newsweek* poll taken shortly after the killings at Kent State, a majority supported the president's invasion of Cambodia. Six out of seven polled said they blamed the students, not the guardsmen, for the killings at Kent State.

Yet a presidential commission appointed to investigate the shootings and other campus unrest concluded that the students had assembled peacefully and that the guard had had no right to attack them. The commission called the shootings "unnecessary, unwarranted, and

A student reacts with horror as a fellow student lies dead, shot by National Guardsmen during a protest in May 1970 at Kent State University in Kent, Ohio. In all, four students were slain.

inexcusable" and continued, "The crisis on American campuses has no parallel in the history of the nation." It seemed to many that the nation was on the brink of a generational civil war.

And, for the first time, war resistance was growing within the government itself. Secretary of the Interior Walter Hickel sent a letter to the president that argued, "If we read history, it clearly shows that youth in its protest must be heard."

"COME IN OUT OF THE DRAFT"

Early in the 1970s, the antiwar movement began to fall into decline. Leaders were frustrated, exhausted, and depressed that the outpouring of public sentiment against the war had made little dent in government policy. Yet there were still young men coming of age who faced the draft, and a new generation of students began to protest the war with renewed energy.

As President Nixon withdrew American troops from Vietnam, draft calls dropped from 17,000 to 10,000 monthly during 1971. But a new system called the lottery added more anxiety for draft-age men. The Selective Service used the lottery to select—at random—the order in which eligible men would be called into the military.

Brian Nerney and his college roommate watched the lottery on TV in December 1969. Selective Service representatives were drawing balls, each labeled with one day of the year, out of a bin. All the eligible men whose birthdays were the same as the first date drawn got number 1. They would be in the first group drafted. Those whose birthdays corresponded to the second ball were drafted second, and so on. Nerney remembered:

> My roommate got number 18 and went to bed, worried and uncertain. Finally, when my birth date didn't come up and didn't come up, I went to bed too. About one in the morning, my father called. "Did you hear your number?" he asked. "It's 343." We were both relieved; we knew Selective Service would take only up to 180 or so.

Meanwhile, men already drafted and fighting in Vietnam took themselves out of the war in larger and larger numbers. "Fragging," the murder of a commanding officer, increased from 1970 to 1971. Desertions occurred three times as often as they had during the Korean War. Writing in the *Armed Forces Journal* in 1971, Marine Colonel Robert Hein said:

> The morale, discipline, and battleworthiness of the U.S. Armed Forces are . . . lower and worse than at any time this century and possibly in the history of the United States. . . . Our army that now remains in Vietnam is in a state approaching collapse.

As the war dragged on and Vietnamization put more of the fighting in the hands of the South Vietnamese army, American soldiers saw less and less reason to stay around and get killed. "Who wants to be the last soldier to die in Vietnam?" was a common question.

When soldiers returned home, the nation did not shower them with parades and respect as it had returning World War II soldiers.

Instead, many Vietnam veterans were shunned or treated with hostility by antiwar protesters and others. After the horrors of the war, readjusting to civilian life was difficult.

Sue Lommen knew several young men who had returned from Vietnam. One "went right ahead and did what was expected of him—made money, built a house." Another came back on drugs and acted violent and crazy. Other veterans expressed their bitterness by joining antiwar protests themselves. One prominent group was Vietnam Veterans against the War.

In early 1971, Vietnam Veterans against the War held hearings at which more than 100 veterans testified to acts of brutality they had committed in Vietnam. Many soldiers had been ordered to kill all the Vietnamese they saw; they had been told to take no prisoners. From the hearings, the veterans planned Dewey Canyon III, a protest to be held in Washington, D.C., in mid-April.

Eleven hundred veterans began the protest by laying wreaths on the Tomb of the Unknown Soldier. They then visited Congress and presented a list of demands, including a demand to end the war. Finally, nearly a thousand veterans threw the medals they had won in Vietnam over the fence surrounding the Capitol steps. Purple Hearts, Silver Stars, the Vietnam Cross of Gallantry, commendation medals— all landed at the feet of the statue of John Marshall, chief justice of the Supreme Court. In the *New York Times,* Jan Barry, who had helped found Vietnam Veterans against the War, wrote:

> To kill on military orders and be a criminal or to refuse to kill and be a criminal is the moral agony of America's Vietnam war generation. It is what has forced upward of sixty thousand young Americans . . . to Canada and has created one hundred thousand military deserters a year in this country and abroad. . . . America's Vietnam generation isn't up against a wall; it's bricked in.

THE MOVEMENT
WAS FED UP!

*I have no secret plan for peace;
I have a public plan.*
　—Senator George McGovern,
　running for president in 1972

In June 1971, Daniel Ellsberg, a former Defense Department employee, gave the *New York Times* a copy of secret Defense Department papers about Vietnam. The *Times* began to publish the so-called "Pentagon Papers," which revealed the deceptions and cover-up that the government had used to keep the country ignorant and misinformed about Vietnam. The papers revealed, as *The Economist* of London noted, that President Johnson had "soft-soaped" the public when he first sent large numbers of troops to Vietnam in 1965, "talking of negotiations when none was in mind, expressing optimism when none was justified."

The Nixon administration tried to stop publication of the papers, but the Supreme Court upheld the right of the *New York Times* to make them public. This decision angered the president so much that he had Ellsberg charged with espionage. Looking for something criminal or damning in Ellsberg's private affairs, Nixon ordered a burglary of Ellsberg's psychiatrist's office and the tapping of Ellsberg's phone.

The disclosure of the government's lies about the war and Nixon's vendetta against Ellsberg horrified many people. By 1971, not only the American people—61 percent in one poll—but also their representatives in Congress were fed up with the war. Several times, members of Congress tried to end the draft and cut off funding for the war, but they never quite succeeded.

NIXON'S SECRET PLAN

Nixon revealed in January 1972 that his administration had started secret peace talks with North Vietnam. The North Vietnamese had offered the same terms that many in Congress and the antiwar movement were proposing: withdrawal of all American troops from Vietnam in exchange for the return of Americans held as prisoners of war (POWs).

The North Vietnamese also wanted the United States to promise it would not disrupt elections in South Vietnam. The elections undoubtedly would defeat the corrupt government of Nguyen Van Thieu, which the United States supported. This last point the Americans were not willing to accept.

As the 1972 presidential election approached, Nixon feared that continuing the war would jeopardize his chance for reelection. The South Vietnamese were not winning in the field, and it looked as if the North Vietnamese would start a major attack around the time of the elections. With these concerns in mind, the president decided to renew the bombing of North Vietnam that President Johnson had stopped in 1968.

When the North Vietnamese attacked, just as the president had feared, Nixon announced that bombing would resume later that month—April 1972. The announcement came as a shock to Americans hopeful for peace.

The bombing had initially been planned for rural areas with few people, but at the last minute Nixon redirected it to the North Vietnamese cities of Hanoi and Haiphong. Hundreds of innocent citizens were killed. Many people began to compare the U.S. government to Hitler's Nazi government in Germany.

Once again, after several years of relative quiet, the nation's campuses erupted with protest—though with a new generation of students. They expressed their horror through marches and rallies; violence escalated on many campuses. At Harvard, students broke into the Center for International Affairs, destroyed offices, and set a fire. When a curfew was set, students smashed windows and broke into university buildings.

University leaders urged students to work within the political system, especially during an election year. But on April 21, 1972, more than 150 colleges and universities went on strike. At the University of Michigan in Ann Arbor, students trashed their ROTC building, tore up documents, and tossed chairs and typewriters out of windows. At Columbia, students occupied buildings and shut down the campus. This time, however, students not taking part in the protests sued the university to resume classes. Eventually, police had to clear student protesters out of the buildings.

Protesters next organized an International Peace Action Day, with demonstrations held around the world. In New York, demonstrators sang "Give Peace a Chance." One man carried a sign that read: "My Son and 45,000 GIs Were Killed in Vietnam in Vain." In another demonstration, protesters tried to pressure Honeywell, a company that made weapons, to stop production of war material. Richard

Fernandez, executive director of Clergy and Laymen Concerned about the War, remembered:

> We talked to them . . . about the [ethical] responsibility of corporations. . . . They said, "In a democracy, when the government asks you to help in an effort like this, we help."

Then one of the protesters asked, "If you had a visit from Washington, would you make gas ovens?" The question was a reference to the gas that Nazis had used to kill Jews during World War II. That question ended the meeting; the Honeywell executives didn't know how to respond.

THE MINING OF HAIPHONG HARBOR

Between June 1969 and the summer of 1972, most American troops were withdrawn from Vietnam. Yet the war was not over. On May 8, 1972, the U.S. government announced that North Vietnamese harbors, mainly Haiphong, would be mined and that the United States would bomb supply lines to China. These aggressive actions flew in the face of the president's promises to end the war, his secret peace talks, and his withdrawal of American troops.

Unplanned, often wild demonstrations again erupted across the country. Demonstrators blocked highways and streets. Even senators and representatives met on the steps of the Capitol to protest the mining. Government offices were crowded with citizens who came to urge Congress to pass legislation against the war.

On the University of Minnesota campus in Minneapolis, students battled police. The protesters threw eggs; police wielded mace and nightsticks. "One side's right, one side's wrong, we're on the side of the Vietcong," chanted the protesters.

"The movement was fed up," said Lester Galt, who took part in the Minnesota protest. "We'd kept hearing about a secret plan to end the war, a secret plan to end the war. We were through." Chants expressed the frustration of many: "If you're gonna have a war there, you're gonna have a war at home."

Dean Zimmermann, who had taken the day off from teaching junior high to protest, grabbed a bullhorn and tried to organize a sit-in behind barricades that closed off Washington Avenue at Oak Street. "The police charged into the intersection, beating savagely," he remembered.

When Dean heard on the police radio, "Get the guy with the bullhorn," he tried to ditch it, but he was jumped by two plainclothes policemen who hit him on the head and maced him. His dog raced after the paddy wagon that carried him to the police station.

As soon as Dean was out on bail, he rejoined the protest. Washington Avenue, a major bus route, was barricaded by protesters for five days. On the second day, Dean remembered, "Crowds spilled over from the campus to Freeway 94 and shut that down, too." By the fifth day, over a thousand people had been arrested.

This protest, along with many others across the country, had finally implemented Henry David Thoreau's vision of civil disobedience—clogging normal activity and bringing business as usual to a standstill.

TALK OF PEACE

The Democratic Convention of 1972 was quite different than that of 1968. For one thing, the ability of the antiwar movement to mount huge, radical protests had ebbed. Furthermore, the Democratic nominee, Senator George McGovern from South Dakota, promoted peace as a major part of his campaign. "I have no secret plan for peace," pledged McGovern at the convention. "I have a public plan." If elected, he intended to stop the bombing in North Vietnam and bring home both troops and prisoners of war within three months.

The Republicans again nominated Richard Nixon, but there were significant protests at this convention, especially by Vietnam veterans who had traveled there in a long caravan across the country. Three veterans in wheelchairs forced their way to the front of the convention hall. "I gave America my all, and the leaders of this government threw me and the others to rot in VA hospitals," Ron Kovic told reporter Roger Mudd in a two-minute interview televised from the convention floor. "What's happening in Vietnam is a crime against humanity." During Nixon's acceptance speech, the veterans yelled "Stop the bombing, stop the war, stop the bombing, stop the war." Kovic remembered thinking:

> They're not going to show [our protest]. . . . They're going to try and hide us like they did in the hospitals. Hundreds of people around us began to clap and shout, "Four more years," trying to drown out our protest. They all seemed very angry and shouted at us to stop.

As the war raged on, veterans began to take part in the protests.

Kovic and his fellow soldiers were removed by Secret Service agents. "I served two tours of duty in Vietnam," he screamed to reporters. "I gave three quarters of my body for America. And what do I get? Spit in the face." Once outside, the three men were locked out. Kovic wondered what else they could do but go home. He sat shaking and crying in his wheelchair.

At the end of October 1972, Secretary of State Henry Kissinger announced that "peace is at hand." At peace talks in Paris, the United States had agreed to end the bombing of North Vietnam and to begin a cease-fire with the North Vietnamese. North Vietnam had agreed to keep Nguyen Van Thieu's government in place in South Vietnam. But Thieu himself refused these compromises. Thus, when Kissinger announced the peace, he was speaking too soon. Soon afterward, Nixon scrapped the agreement.

The fall of 1972 was quiet for the peace movement, except for the Indochina Peace Campaign (IPC), an action started by Tom Hayden and his companion, actress Jane Fonda. First came a speaking tour by Hayden and Fonda to educate people in states important to George McGovern's bid for the presidency. Though minor violence and disruption marred some events, Fonda and Hayden, along with singer Holly Near, were enthusiastically received in Illinois, New Jersey, and Ohio. What touched them most was seeing "people change before our eyes. . . . I saw a young Nixon campaign worker remove his button," said Hayden. The pair urged people to pressure Nixon to sign the Paris peace agreement.

But the antiwar movement still couldn't put a candidate in office. In November 1972, Richard Nixon was reelected with 60.7 percent of the vote.

NO SILENT NIGHT IN VIETNAM

With the election out of the way, the Nixon administration tried to convince Nguyen Van Thieu to accept the terms of the peace agreement. In a secret message, Nixon told Thieu that the United States would continue to support him, and the president showed this support by again ordering the mining of Haiphong harbor and new bombings of Haiphong and Hanoi.

For 12 days around Christmas, the United States pursued the heaviest bombing of the war. North Vietnamese factories, train stations, and homes were destroyed. Hanoi's chief hospital was bombed, and doctors had to amputate people's limbs to free them from the wreckage.

At the time, singer Joan Baez was in Hanoi delivering Christmas mail to the American POWs. Walking through the city, she passed people wearing white headbands to symbolize the death of relatives. She remembered one woman "sitting on a small heap of rubble, pounding her fists on her thighs and crying with a despair that was ferocious." The fear of being hit by the bombs herself made Baez want to vomit.

At home, what came to be called the Christmas bombing threw antiwar protesters into despair—and action. Thousands held vigils at shopping centers and churches. In New York City, demonstrators stopped traffic for hours. Some protesters raised money to help rebuild the Hanoi hospital. Others sent the White House a Christmas tree—its branches and ornaments broken. A banner raised outside Radio City Music Hall in New York read, "There's No Silent Night in Vietnam."

American newspapers also came down hard on the government. The *St. Louis Post-Dispatch* called the bombing "new madness." Congress responded with resolutions to end armed action in Vietnam as soon as the POWs were returned. Finally, on December 29, hearing the outpouring for peace, Richard Nixon stopped the bombing of North Vietnam.

The Paris peace talks resumed, and on January 23, 1973, Henry Kissinger and North Vietnamese leader Le Duc Tho signed an agreement. It said that a cease-fire would begin in four days. All American troops in Vietnam—some 27,000—would be withdrawn and all POWs returned in two months. The Thieu government and the interim North Vietnamese government would have equal control of

South Vietnam; and, when the two parties settled their differences, North and South Vietnam would be reunited.

AFTER THE PEACE

Although the Paris peace agreement did end the war in Vietnam, it did not mean an end to antiwar activity. Largely through the Indochina Peace Campaign, activists pressured Nixon to live up to the peace agreement. They raised money to help Vietnamese people whose lives had been shattered by the war. They also pressured Congress and the president to grant amnesty to American war resisters who had been jailed or had left the country for Canada.

Then, on August 9, 1974, Richard Nixon resigned as president of the United States. A scandal called Watergate—which involved the illegal entering and wiretapping of Democratic Party headquarters in Washington, D.C.—had brought Nixon to the brink of impeachment.

Nixon's successor, Gerald Ford, continued to support the Thieu government in South Vietnam. But Congress rejected South Vietnam's request for additional military aid. Thieu had little support from his own troops against increasing North Vietnamese pressure, and his government fell in April 1975. North Vietnamese tanks rolled into the capital city of Saigon.

The North Vietnamese controlled all of Vietnam. They renamed Saigon, calling it Ho Chi Minh City in honor of their leader, who had recently died. Helicopters rescued U.S. embassy personnel. Vietnam was united, and the Americans were finally gone.

LESSONS LEARNED

The antiwar protesters had taught the country many lessons. They had challenged Americans to rethink patriotism, resistance, leadership, and obligation. As the movement grew, it built a bridge between regions, generations, and social and economic divisions.

The Vietnam War itself, the longest war in American history, had also taught Americans some lessons. They never wanted to endure an-

A POW greets his wife and children upon returning home from imprisonment in North Vietnam.

other conflict like it. No longer would the United States be so quick to intervene in the politics of other nations. No longer would the American government pay so little heed to the voices of its own citizens.

After the war, the government took steps toward reconciliation with the antiwar protesters. In 1973, the draft was ended and the U.S. military became a voluntary force. The U.S. government still had cases pending against thousands of draft resisters. But in September 1974, President Ford offered resisters amnesty if they performed two years of community service. On January 21, 1977, President Jimmy Carter issued a general pardon for all draft resisters.

Two soldiers visit the Vietnam War Memorial in Washington, D.C.
The wall contains the names of the estimated 58,191 Americans who died
in Vietnam.

The United States government also began to help those whose lives had been shattered by the fighting in Vietnam. The country opened its doors to many Vietnamese, Cambodians, and other Southeast Asians left homeless by the war.

Finally, the country began to address the damage to its own soldiers from Vietnam. Movies such as *The Deer Hunter, Apocalypse Now, In Country,* and *Born on the Fourth of July* chronicled the war and its effect on soldiers who returned home with lasting emotional wounds.

A WALL OF LOSS AND HEALING

On Veterans Day, November 13, 1982, Maya Ying Lin's Vietnam War Memorial was dedicated in Washington, D.C. Vietnam veterans and thousands of citizens had raised money for the memorial as a way to pay tribute to the soldiers who had died in Vietnam. It was time for Americans to reconcile their differences about the war.

Maya Ying Lin, a 21-year-old architecture student at Yale University, had envisioned the memorial as a wall cut into the earth. She designed an elegant sweep of dark granite set into a low hillside, incised with the names of the 58,191 Americans who died in Vietnam.

After the wall was dedicated, National Park Service rangers helped visitors take rubbings of names at the wall. Those who had lost sons, fathers, brothers, cousins, or friends in the war could take home tangible evidence that the nation had honored their loved ones. The memorial also offered people a chance to reflect on the meaning of the war. As visitors looked at the polished stone, they could see themselves reflected back, overlaid with the names of the dead. Thus the memorial mirrored the experiences of all Americans, bringing together those who had lived and those who had died.

Plasma is given to a wounded soldier while one of his comrades, **right,** *races into battle.* **Opposite page:** *A South Vietnamese farm girl carries on with her work in a rice field while South Vietnamese soldiers march through in search of snipers.*

SELECTED BIBLIOGRAPHY

Appy, Christian G. *Working Class War: American Combat Soldiers and Vietnam.* Chapel Hill, North Carolina: University of North Carolina Press, 1993.

DeBenedetti, Charles. *An American Ordeal: The Antiwar Movement of the Vietnam Era.* Syracuse, New York: Syracuse University Press, 1990.

Gershon Gottlieb, Sherry. *Hell No, We Won't Go! Resisting the Draft During the Vietnam War.* New York: Viking, 1991.

Gioglio, Gerald. *Days of Decision: An Oral History of Conscientious Objectors in the Military during the Vietnam War.* Trenton, N.J.: Broken Rifle Press, 1989.

Hayden, Tom. *Reunion: A Memoir.* New York: Random House, 1988.

Herring, George C. *LBJ and Vietnam: A Different Kind of War.* Austin, Texas: University of Texas Press, 1994.

Isserman, Maurice. *The Vietnam War.* New York: Facts on File, 1992.

Kotash, Myrna. *Long Way from Home: The Story of the Sixties Generation in Canada.* Toronto: James Lorimer & Company, 1980.

Kovic, Ron. *Born on the Fourth of July.* New York: Pocket Books, 1976.

Lynd, Alice, ed., *We Won't Go: Personal Accounts of War Objectors.* Boston: Beacon Press, 1968.

Marrin, Albert. *America and Vietnam: The Elephant and the Tiger.* New York: Viking Press, 1992.

Sale, Kirkpatrick. *SDS.* New York: Vintage Books, 1974.

Santoli, Al. *Everything We Had.* New York: Random House, 1981.

Schulzinger, Robert D. *Time for War: The United States and Vietnam, 1941–1975.* New York: Oxford University Press, 1977.

Small, Melvin, and William D. Hoover, eds., *Give Peace a Chance.* Syracuse, New York: Syracuse University Press, 1992.

Smith, Winnie. *American Daughter Gone to War.* New York: Pocket Books, 1992.

VanDeMark, Brian. *Into the Quagmire: Lyndon Johnson and the Escalation of the Vietnam War.* New York: Oxford University Press, 1991.

Van Devanter, Lynda and Joan Furey, eds., *Visions of War, Visions of Peace: Writings of Women in the Vietnam War.* New York: Warner Books, 1991.

Warren, James. *Portrait of a Tragedy: America and the Vietnam War.* New York: Lothrop, Lee and Shepard Books, 1990.

Wells, Tom. *The War Within: America's Battle over Vietnam.* Berkeley: University of California Press, 1994.

Willenson, Kim, ed., *The Bad War: An Oral History of the Vietnam War.* New York: New American Library, 1987.

Wolff, Tobias. *In Pharoah's Army.* New York: Random House, 1994.

Zaroulis, Nancy and Gerald Sullivan. *Who Spoke Up: American Protest Against the War in Vietnam, 1963–1975.* New York: Doubleday & Company, Inc., 1984.

Flag burning was a common form of protest during the conflict in Vietnam.

INDEX

ACKNOWLEDGMENTS

Photographs and illustrations used with permission of UPI/Corbis-Bettmann, 2, 6, 12, 14, 24, 32, 37, 40, 44, 48, 55, 62, 79, 80, 82; © Phillips Bourns, 9; Corbis/Bettmann-UPI, 13, 51, 67, 70, 83; © Jason Lauré, 17, 52; Santi Visalli Inc./ Archive Photos, 20, 47; National Archives, 28, 29, Archive Photos, 43; Swarthmore College Peace Collection, 38, 59, 75; New York Daily News Photo, 85.

Front cover, Jason Lauré (top left, top right); Archive Photos (center)
Back cover, Archive Photos